Original title:
The Shoreline of Serenity

Copyright © 2025 Creative Arts Management OÜ
All rights reserved.

Author: Juliette Kensington
ISBN HARDBACK: 978-1-80581-632-4
ISBN PAPERBACK: 978-1-80581-159-6
ISBN EBOOK: 978-1-80581-632-4

Trails of Soft Footprints

Waves tickle toes, what a sight,
Seagulls wheek, take flight,
Sandcastles lean, then fall down,
Oh, the joys of a sandy crown!

Crabs dancing sideways, oh so sly,
Shells whisper secrets, passing by,
Flip-flops flop, a comical bounce,
Laughter echoes, watch us pronounce!

Beach balls soaring, dodged with flair,
Lost my hat, it's floating in air,
Sunblock's sticky, glistening glow,
Sandy snacks, oh, don't let them go!

Footprints lead where giggles run,
Chasing dreams in the bright sun,
Fishy faces, splashes galore,
This funny place, who could ask for more?

Secrets Beneath the Surface

Bubbles rise and fish take flight,
The mermaids laugh, what a sight!
Seashells whisper silly jokes,
While crabs wear hats, amusing folks.

Octopuses play hide and seek,
With a wink and a little peek.
Starfish dance with silly flair,
While seahorses twirl through salty air.

Ocean's Embrace

The waves call out, 'Come join the fun!'
Flipping on surfboards under the sun.
Seagulls squawk a cheeky tune,
While dolphins laugh, a jumping boon.

Sandcastles rise with humor bold,
Royal moats of water, cold!
Nearby, a crab has lost his throne,
Its crown's a soda cap, alone.

Dawn's Gentle Light

The sun peeks up with sleepy yawn,
A crab complains, 'Must we go on?'
Seashells snicker as they glow,
While jellyfish do the morning show.

Fish in tuxedos swim by fast,
Who knew that dawn can be such a blast?
The turtlenecks of sea turtles stretch,
'Fashionable' is what they sketch!

Waves of Contentment

A surfboard rides on laughter's crest,
The ocean frolics, feeling blessed.
Mermaid's giggles, a playful sound,
As fishy friends swirl all around.

Seaweed's tickle brings a smile,
While crabs compete in a dance style.
A group of fish trade knock-knock jokes,
In this watery world, joy evoked.

Traces of a Gentle Tide

Waves tell secrets in a blur,
Seagulls squawk with a goofy slur.
A crab wears shoes that are too tight,
He scuttles off in a comical flight.

Flip-flops dance in the salty breeze,
Chasing a seagull with such ease.
There's laughter echoing, pure and bright,
As a kid builds castles that take to flight.

Visions from the Edge of the World

At the cliff, the wind does tease,
Making my hair jump like a sneeze.
Seashells giggle when you pick them up,
And a fish just gave my toes a sup.

With a wink, the horizon winks back,
A dolphin's in on the comedy act.
Waves scatter jokes across the swell,
While I laugh awkwardly, what a tale to tell.

A Canvas of Coral and Sand

The beach is painted in clownish hues,
Where jellyfish wear the silliest shoes.
Each wave crashes with a playful shout,
While crabs engage in a silly bout.

The starfish, they argue over the sun,
'Who's brightest here, it's all just for fun!'
Bikini tops fly like flags on parade,
As laughter fills the seaside charade.

Cradled by the Ocean's Arms

Rocking gently, the water sways,
While beach balls bounce in a wacky craze.
Seashells sing songs of the dumbest sort,
And sandcastles fight in a dandy court.

A beach towel flops like a tired dog,
While a kid plays tag with a beachy fog.
Each splash sounds like giggles in the sun,
Life's a carnival, and we're not done!

Serene Twilight

As the sun sets with a quirky grin,
Seagulls dance while the crabs spin.
The waves whisper jokes from afar,
While starfish giggle, 'We're the real stars!'

Shells confide secrets to the sand,
Waves laugh out loud, oh so grand.
The horizon stretches, yawns and sighs,
As a beach ball thinks it can touch the skies.

Glimmers of Dawn

Morning light brings a ticklish breeze,
Tickling toes, as it pleases.
Fish in the water are making a splash,
Above, in the clouds, a kite takes a dash.

Crabs hold a meeting, plotting their take,
On a sandcastle plan, they all will partake.
With a fork and a spoon, they'll dig and they'll play,
Who knew morning could be this way?

Land of Quiet Reflection

Here lies a spot where the ducks quack tunes,
Under the gaze of the lazy moons.
Turtles play chess with seaweed as their board,
While otters concoct a prank, oh my word!

A clam yells, 'Let's have a dance-off tonight!'
But the jellyfish just glows, feeling quite bright.
In the background, a crab is trying to groove,
With a soft rhythm, it starts to move.

Floating on Still Waters

Bobbing along on a leaf with glee,
A frog wearing shades feels so carefree.
Dragonflies giggle, darting about,
While a fish jokes, 'Why are you all out?'

In the calm, there's a splash, oh what a sight!
A duck slips and slides, oh what a fright!
As the sun glimmers and laughter rolls in,
Even the quietest day can have a grin!

Visions of Calm Waters

Waves whisper secrets, a fish in a hat,
Splashing the crabs, who all laugh at that.
Seagulls on vacation, sipping on juice,
Chasing the showers, oh what a truce!

Pebbles in pockets, a sandcastle queen,
Looking for seashells—she's lost in the scene.
Laughter is echoing under the sun,
With flip-flops flying, we're all on the run!

Between Sea and Sky

Clouds make great pillows, just float on by,
Sprinkling raindrops, a sweet lullaby.
Kites take the lead, while we munch on fries,
A seagull's a thief with a gleam in his eyes.

In this wacky world, where the sun likes to play,
A dolphin dances—who knew it could sway?
We ponder and ponder, then dive without fear,
Splashing in giggles, the horizon is near!

Dance of the Coasting Clouds

Clouds wear a tutu, they flounce in the breeze,
While sailboats yodel, sailing with ease.
The sun throws a party, come help with the pie,
While crabs do the cha-cha, oh me, oh my!

Waves play the trumpet, all on their own,
The seashells they sing, a remarkable tone.
Together we twirl, 'neath the wide, wavy sky,
Life's just a beach ball—let's give it a try!

Sheltered in Serenity

Picnics with penguins, who brought the cheese?
They honk and they wiggle—this party's a breeze!
Under umbrellas, the jellyfish glide,
With laughter and lemonade, oh what a ride!

A crab on a skateboard rolls past with a wink,
His shell's looking sharp; it's all in the blink.
We lounge with our jokes in a sunbeam's embrace,
Finding joy in the silly, this magical place!

Solace of the Shells

On the beach where sand meets the sea,
Shells giggle as they dance with glee.
A starfish plays peek-a-boo,
While crabs do the cha-cha too!

Seagulls argue over chips,
While surfers catch breeze with their flips.
Bubbles pop like tiny balloons,
In this land of aquatic cartoons.

Tide pools hold secrets untold,
Where seaweed wraps like a green scarf bold.
An octopus flips pancakes with flair,
Making breakfast in water, beyond compare!

At sundown, the waves start their dance,
Even sea turtles join in the prance.
With laughter echoing through the air,
Shells become storytellers, everywhere!

Where Peace Resides

In a cove where laughter's the norm,
A jellyfish wears a bright floral form.
Starfish discuss their beauty tips,
While sea urchins hold stylish quips.

Sandcastles rise with a mighty cheer,
As crabs throw a beach party near.
Seagulls flit for the beach snack trade,
Swapping tater chips in a grand parade.

Parents lounge under umbrellas wide,
While kids on boogie boards glide.
Sand in shoes and splashes around,
In this peaceful chaos, joy is found!

When day turns to dusk, and stars appear,
The waves whisper secrets for all to hear.
Laughter echoes, not a single frown,
In this paradise, no need to drown!

Harmonious Horizon

Where wind blows gentle, laughs unfold,
The sun steals the spotlight, pure gold.
Dolphins leap and dance in the air,
While sea otters giggle without a care.

Beach umbrellas sway to the beat,
While flip-flops mingle, oh, what a feat!
Children sculpt their dreams in the sand,
While crabs lend a helping hand.

Every wave whispers a silly tale,
Fish in costumes start to set sail.
Pirate parrots squawk and squabble,
While seashells play in a soft bubble.

As stars twinkle in the night's embrace,
The ocean sings of every place.
Sandcastle monarchs rule the shore,
In this joyful haven, forevermore!

Symphony of the Tide

Listen close to the ocean's lilt,
A jellybean tide with soft froth built.
Fish in tuxedos glide in style,
While crabs moonwalk, oh what a file!

Seashells tap dance on the wet sand,
Tidal waves join a merry band.
Sand dollars wear shades, living grand,
As the seagulls choreograph the strand.

A conch shell plays a sweet serenade,
Dancing squid create a colorful parade.
Wind whispers jokes through sea grass bends,
In this ocean giggle, happiness extends.

As the sun dips low in the salty air,
Waves bow gracefully without a care.
With laughter wrapped in the ocean's tide,
Here's where the souls joyfully abide!

Driftwood Chronicles

On the beach, a log does sway,
Wondering what it's seen today.
A fish shouts, 'You're just a seat!'
While crabs compete for a tasty treat.

Seagulls plan their next big heist,
Stealing chips, oh, isn't that nice?
A teenage whale swims by, quite spry,
Waving 'hi' with a splashy sigh.

The sun plays peek-a-boo with clouds,
While beachgoers cheer in their crowds.
Forgotten shovels, lost in the sand,
Prepare for battles, oh so unplanned!

Oh, driftwood, you'll tell tales galore,
Of sunken ships and treasures in store.
But here you sit, and that's a bummer,
Just another piece of ocean's slumber!

Life at Water's Edge

Life by the sea, what a strange place,
Where jellyfish dance with such grace.
Flip-flops lost in a crab's quick snap,
Creating laughter, making the map.

Sandcastles rise with great ambition,
Only to face a tide's cruel mission.
Children giggle, water's so cold,
Splashes and shrieks, pure joy to behold!

A dog races by, with waves in tow,
The seagulls laugh, putting on a show.
Sunburned tourists, color like lobster,
Sipping drinks, acting like mobsters!

The sun sets low, casting shadows wide,
As seashells whisper what they hide.
Life's silly moments, we won't forget,
At the water's edge, where we laugh yet!

Raindrops on the Ocean

Raindrops giggle as they hit the sea,
Playing tag with waves, happy and free.
Clouds look down, what a silly sight,
Dancing their jig in the fading light.

A fish pokes out, wearing a hat,
Confused by the weather, imagine that!
He hops in the air, lands back with grace,
Splashing a jelly, who's lost in space?

Umbrellas flip, oh what a scene,
Like chickens fleeing, all fluffed and mean.
A surfboard slides on the slickened sand,
While giggling shrimp form a marching band.

As rain subsides, the laughter stays,
With water's edge offering playful rays.
Each droplet tells stories of fun and cheer,
As we dance to the waves, year after year!

Horizon of Dreams

Out where dreams and waters meet,
A dolphin's waltz, isn't that neat?
With flip-flops flying, people applaud,
As waves crash down, all gnarly and flawed.

The sunsets paint the sky in fun,
While seagulls argue, 'I'm number one!'
They squawk about the best fish around,
While the ocean chuckles, adding its sound.

Kids run wild, shrieking in glee,
As sand envelops their tiny knees.
A treasure map drawn in a puddle of dreams,
Leads to candy, or so it seems!

With beach balls flying and laughter spread,
There's joy in the air, laughter ahead.
So here's to the horizon, wild and deep,
Where every wave promises fun to keep!

Silence Wrapped in Seafoam

The seagulls squawk, a beach parade,
They steal my fries; I'm quite dismayed.
I tried to build a mighty sand tower,
    But it fell apart within the hour.

The crabs in suits, they waltz with glee,
    In tiny pinches, they challenge me.
With every wave, they misbehave,
Plotting schemes as they dig and cave.

My sunburn's red, a tomato's plight,
The sunscreen missed; I've lost the fight.
A beach ball lands upon my head,
I laugh aloud, "At least I'm fed!"

The ocean laughs, it knows my shame,
And waves a hand, plays its funny game.

Dancers of the Dusk

As the sun dips low, it casts its spell,
The crabs do a jig, you can't quite tell.
With flips and flops, their dance is grand,
Who knew crabs could form a band?

A seagull dressed in feathered flair,
Twirls past a child without a care.
"Change your game!" he seems to say,
"You'll never get a tan this way!"

The sand's too hot; the flip-flops squeak,
As laughter echoes down the creek.
Fish chase dreams of a wiggly worm,
While kids giggle and twist and squirm.

The twilight whispers, "Silly scene,
A dance-off here, where none are mean!"
In waves of joy, the shoreline sways,
As evening winks and starts to play.

Where Waves Meet Whispered Thoughts

A gentle breeze, I sit and muse,
But then a wave drags off my shoes.
My thoughts are caught in watery thrills,
While seaweed wraps around my heels.

Conversations with a beach-old sock,
It tells me tales of the ocean clock.
I nod along, pretend to care,
While every wave steals summer air.

The tides conspire, they plot their schemes,
As fish burst forth from sneaky dreams.
They splash my jeans with giggly glee,
And grin at mortals—they're so free!

Whispers of laughter fill the air,
Where mermaids pass with salty flair.
"Come join our fun!" the ocean calls,
While I just stand and watch the brawls.

Skylines and Shorelines

The city meets the ocean's grin,
With boats and jets that spin and spin.
I wave at fish in fancy hats,
As seagulls gossip like old spats.

The skyline glimmers, a cocktail hour,
But here the jellyfish have the power.
With breezy jumps, they float and glide,
While I trip on a flip-flop slide.

Umbrellas turn like wild-eyed kites,
Chasing after pleasure's lights.
Sandcastles rise like wannabe kings,
But watch as the tide, with mischief, springs.

"Best of luck!" the ocean shouts,
As I paddle past the gremlin's bouts.
Laughter trickles like shells on the floor,
In this zany dance, who could ask for more?

Coastal Reflections

Seagulls squawk and steal my fries,
While friendly crabs wear silly ties.
Waves crash down, they playfully splash,
I dodge the foam, oh what a clash!

Shells all gleam like tiny spoons,
I ponder if they'd playcartoon tunes.
Under the sun, my hat's on tight,
It's a beach party, oh what a sight!

Sunburned noses tell their tales,
Of surfboards wiped out, dolphin fails.
Yet laughter echoes through the foam,
In wild waves, we still find home.

Sandy toes and sugary treats,
Building castles, life's simple feats.
With every roar and every cheer,
This crazy shore brings endless cheer.

Beneath the Sail

A pirate ship with a veggie crew,
Cabbage sails with a leafy view.
Carrots shout, "We're off to loot!"
While pickles dance in their green boots.

Wind whips up, and sails go boom,
Tomatoes scream from below deck's gloom.
Out on the waves, we'make some waves,
Sailing forth like crunchy braves!

Fishy friends wave with fins in glee,
Joining in on our veggie spree.
Life at sea can get quite wild,
Just ask our cheese, it's quite reviled!

As sunset paints the sky with flair,
We laugh aloud, who needs a chair?
Under stars, we'll cook and sway,
Veggies rule, hip-hip hooray!

Driftwood Dreams

Driftwood dances, oh what a sight,
Wobbly wonders in fading light.
Seashell gossip, a conch shell sings,
About the mischief that driftwood brings.

A crab with swagger struts along,
His tiny claws are a tap dance song.
In this driftwood world of unique flair,
A catfish jokes from his sandy lair.

We gather 'round to share strange quests,
Like finding a shoe in the ocean's nests.
With every laugh, our worries thin,
On this sandy stage, let the fun begin!

So here we sit, with friends galore,
Counting treasures that wash ashore.
With driftwood dreams and chuckles light,
Life on the beach feels just right.

Whispering Waves

Whispers murmur from the rolling sea,
Tickling toes, "Come dance with me!"
The waves play games, they crash and tease,
A playful push, with such great ease.

The sunbathers giggle, sand in their hair,
While ice cream melts beyond repair.
Seagulls swoop down, grab a bite,
Oh! That's my sandwich? What a plight!

A floaty unicorn just drifted by,
With a rainbow tail, oh my, oh my!
Children squeal and join the fun,
Chasing bubbles until they run.

As twilight nears, we gather close,
Sharing tales from our beachy hosts.
With salty air and hearts so brave,
We cherish each laugh the ocean gave.

Elysian Beaches

Sandy toes and seagull's call,
A crab scuttles, no care at all.
Sunburnt noses, ice cream smears,
Giggles echo, with no fears.

Kites dipped low, they dance and glide,
A sandwich thief, the seagull pride.
Waves chase kids, oh what a race,
Splashing laughter fills the space.

Tanning lotion, a slippery mess,
Oops, fell in, I must confess!
Flips and flops from waves so wide,
Soon I'll be a beach bum's guide.

But as the sun begins to fade,
I spot the jellyfish parade.
A beach ball whacks my friend right silly,
We laugh 'til we ache, oh what a filly!

Radiance of Dusk

As dusk unfolds, the hues collide,
A dolphin jumps, with joyous pride.
Flip-flop fights between the friends,
With silly bets, the laughter blends.

The sunset sings a golden song,
While sandcastles stand proud and strong.
My cola spilled, it bubbles high,
A fizzy fountain! Oh my, oh my!

Starfish battles, who'll take the prize?
We trade our snacks and roll our eyes.
With twilight's cloak, in waves we dip,
But watch your step, or you might trip!

As night arrives, it's time to roast,
Marshmallows for the s'mores, we boast.
Giggle fits as flames go wild,
Who knew serenity could be so wild?

Salted Serenity

Salt upon our tongues so sweet,
With every wave, we skip and beat.
A crab and I, we share a stare,
He scuttles quick, I grin and dare.

Umbrellas flip in the sudden breeze,
Tanning gone wrong—oh, what a tease!
Friends doing cannonballs with style,
In perfect sync, we swim a mile.

A seagull steals my fries away,
I chase him down, it's all in play.
The ocean whispers, waves in tow,
But watch your drink, it's on the go!

Laughter rings, it's not a bore,
Chasing tides upon the shore.
A sunset toast, with snacks we cheer,
In this silly bliss, we shed our fear!

Canvas of Calm

Brush of sea and painted sky,
A canvas where the gulls can fly.
With laughter bright like morning light,
We dance along the water's bite.

Kites decide to take a dive,
My sandwich, oh no! It's not alive!
Rolls and tumbles, our day's delight,
While sunscreen fights the sun's strong bite.

Picnic feasts turn into games,
We take turns yelling funny names.
Yet as the tide begins to crest,
There's always time for one more jest.

Dusk wraps softly, drawing night,
We gather close, the fire's bright.
With waves and jokes, we bid adieu,
This silly shore will wait for you!

Driftwood Lullabies

On a beach of mismatched socks,
Seagulls squawk like clocks.
A crab performs a little jig,
While kids argue over a twig.

The tide rolls in with a whoosh,
Surfboards beauty with a woosh.
A fish takes flight, oh what a sight,
As laughter dances into the night.

Stars descend like falling bread,
While starfish plot in their head.
Koalas on kayaks float by,
Winking at the moon in the sky.

Find a sandcastle with a moat,
Alien fish, ready to gloat.
As shellfish play a melody,
Serenity's a comedy at sea!

The Palette of Peaceful Waters

Colors splash on the ocean's edge,
A turtle trying to make a pledge.
"I'll swim faster than the wind!" he boasts,
As jellyfish prepare their ghostly toasts.

A Pelican wearing a stylish hat,
Sips lemonade while chasing a cat.
Bubbles rise with a silly song,
While beach balls bounce all day long.

Crabs play tag, oh what a sight,
Scurrying left and dashing right.
An octopus spins jellybeans,
Dancing under disco beams.

Waves break softly with a giggle,
As laughter makes the sandwiggle.
The fish hold a joke-telling fest,
In this colorful watery nest!

Whispers of the Tides

The tide tells a secret, oh so sly,
As waves chuckle and fish wink an eye.
Shells conspire, plotting a scheme,
To steal the spotlight and reign supreme.

A dolphin wearing a party hat,
Finds a floating cat who thinks he's fat.
Jellyfish giggle, lighting the scene,
As mermaids play hopscotch; what a routine!

Sand crabs are having a crabby dance,
In the moonlight, they take a chance.
"Watch me twirl!" one proudly declares,
While everyone laughs at the silly stares.

Seagulls wearing sunglasses glide,
As the laughter beats like the tide.
Each wave whispers tales of fun,
Under the bright, inviting sun!

Calm Between the Waves

The sea waits for a silly pun,
As waves play tag and have their fun.
A clam with glasses reads a book,
While octopuses steal a look.

A beach ball bounces, oh so round,
While flip-flops tumble on the ground.
Each laugh echoes across the bay,
As seagulls imitate in a cheeky play.

The lifeguard's got a dog on a board,
As beachcombers shout, "We're so bored!"
A sunburned crab rolls in the sand,
Creating art, oh isn't it grand?

In the calm found here between the swells,
Laughter intertwines, and joy compels.
Though tidal waves may come and go,
In fun-filled moments, we all glow!

Serenity in Blue

Waves roll in with a giggle,
Seagulls dive in a wiggle.
Sandcastles tugged by the tide,
Shells laughing as they hide.

Flip-flops flop, a funny dance,
A crab sneaks in for a glance.
Laughter bubbles from the shore,
As surfboards crash with a roar.

Children splash with puddly glee,
While seaweed wraps up like a key.
Breezes tease and swirl around,
Silliness is where it's found.

The sun drops low, like a clown,
As sunset paints the skies brown.
All creatures laugh, from fish to pup,
In this place, joy's filling up.

Gentle Caress of the Ocean

Ocean waves with a gentle laugh,
Tickle toes on their watery path.
A jellyfish does a wobbly jig,
While crabs march in, tiny and big.

Sunbathers wear hats two sizes too wide,
As wind takes their snacks for a ride.
Beach chairs topple in a fit,
While sunscreen spreads too much bit.

Sandy sandwiches fly with glee,
As seagulls plot a daring spree.
Here, laughter is a daily quest,
As waves come in and disrupt the rest.

Splashes echo like a call,
While funny hats trip and fall.
In this spot, fun never stalls,
As the sun bids farewell and twirls.

Horizon's Quiet Embrace

The horizon yawns in quiet delight,
As dolphins put on a splashy sight.
Upside-down boats spin their tale,
While beach balls bounce without fail.

Fluffy clouds are cotton candy,
While kids run wild, oh so handy.
Kites dance high and then they dive,
Chasing seagulls, they come alive.

Flip a towel, it flies away,
Like a bird, in cheerful play.
Everyone's smiling, the sun's a prank,
As waves giggle and join the rank.

Even the shoreline, in laughter, dips,
While seashells wear silly lips.
In this place of peaceful sounds,
Joyful chaos knows no bounds.

Stillness at Water's Edge

By water's edge, a calm retreat,
Where fish perform a splashing feat.
Turtles trot in a slow parade,
While sandcastles aren't afraid to fade.

A picnic blanket flutters about,
With ants debating on a route.
Birds take turns to dive and dash,
As umbrellas flip with a crashing clash.

Shells spin tales of salty lore,
While waves giggle and ask for more.
A cool breeze tickles every cheek,
And laughter dances, oh so sleek.

As the day whispers its goodbye,
And fireflies flicker in the sky.
Stillness here is a funny tease,
In this joyful beachside breeze.

A Retreat from Time

Waves giggle, snatch my shoes,
Seagulls squawk, I didn't choose.
Sandcastles made with utmost care,
Crab migrations, a seaside fair.

Tide comes in, my snack's a goner,
Sandy face, I'm quite the loner.
Laughing shells, they mock my plight,
Fish are dancing, oh what a sight!

I chase a breeze, yet it won't play,
Salt on my lips, where's my beret?
Koalas surf with utmost flair,
Whispers of joy filled in the air.

At dusk, I dine on crab-stuffed pies,
Jellyfish waltz, oh how time flies!
Life's a beach, with giggles in tow,
Silly moments, a lively show.

Moments of Tranquility

Greet the sun with pancake dreams,
Waves tickle toes, or so it seems.
Laughing at seagulls flying low,
Chasing shadows, to and fro.

Tango with a wayward kite,
Beachballs bouncing, what a sight!
Surfers shout, I try to dance,
With my flip-flops, I take a chance.

Sand gets stuck in every crack,
I find my drink, wait, where's the snack?
Shells perform a slapstick show,
Nature's jest, I'm in the flow.

Peacefully swaying, then—oh wow!
A fish just winked, can you tell how?
Moments tickle, laughter's the key,
Tranquility with jests, oh what glee!

Sails in the Breeze

Sails hoist up with goofy grins,
Wind's a prankster, where it spins.
Laughing boats in a jolly race,
Crabs in tuxedos join the chase.

Oyster jokes in the brine, all right,
Who knew the sea's such a delight?
Chasing waves like dreamy dreams,
Swabs with hats, oh the memes!

Mariners swap their silly tales,
As dolphins flip through salty gales.
Anchors away, but where's the map?
Fishy humor brings a clap.

Stars at night make wishes sly,
We toast to dreams beneath the sky.
Sailing home with belly laughs,
Breezy bliss, our friendly halves.

Nature's Resting Place

Bumbles in the grass, oh my dear,
Nature's giggles, we all can hear.
Butterflies join the silly flight,
Bouncing blooms, "Take that, sunlight!"

Squirrels debate their favorite nuts,
Chattering wildly, just little ruts.
Beehives buzzing with funny quirks,
Nature's laughter, where joy lurks.

Turtles race in a dainty style,
Seaweed wigs make the dolphins smile.
Aquatic pranks on this fine day,
Fauna frolics in a zany way.

Under trees where shadows play,
We giggle time calmly away.
Nature's ropes have tied us tight,
In humor wrapped, we find delight.

Sunsets and Stillness

The sun dips low in a fiery glow,
Seagulls squawk, trying to steal the show.
A crab in shorts creeps by, quite bold,
Waving its claws, a comedic mold.

Beach balls bounce with giggles and squeals,
Flip-flops flying, oh, how it appeals.
People stumble, tripping with pride,
On cream-filled donuts, hoping to glide.

A sandcastle built, but it quickly goes down,
As waves crash hard, while we all frown.
The tide returns, claiming its space,
While we chase our dreams in this sandy race.

Laughter erupts like the splash of the sea,
In this joyful chaos, we feel so free.
Under a blanket of stars, we unite,
Chasing the whims of the playful night.

The Breath of Morning Mist

The dawn breaks soft with a tickle of air,
A seagull claps while locals stare.
Coffee spills while we wiggle our toes,
As morning mist plays with the nose.

Waves whisper secrets to the shore,
A dog goes diving, oh what a chore!
A startled fish jumps, making a splash,
While we spill our breakfast with one goofy crash.

The beachland yoga class tries to please,
But sand in your shorts? Oh goodness, jeez!
Twisting and turning, in pure disarray,
With laughter rising as we all sway.

That's how we breathe in the soft morning charm,
With giggles and snacks, and no need for calm.
So here's to the mornings that keep us awake,
With clouds of laughter and cake afterbreak.

Pebbles of Time

Collecting pebbles, each one unique,
Eyes on the ground, it's treasure we seek.
A blue one winks while a red one sneers,
They whisper tales of our silly fears.

The tide rolls in, stealing our prize,
While a sand crab laughs, to our surprise.
With buckets full of hopes that don't quite fit,
We ponder the value of each tiny bit.

Splashing in puddles, we giggle and dance,
As a jellyfish blunders, giving us a chance.
To watch the mighty waves tumble and roar,
While we gather our treasures right back to the shore.

Time ticks away like grains in the sand,
With memories formed, all beautifully planned.
In this jester's play, we embrace the silly,
Finding friendship in nature, so warm and frilly.

In the Embrace of the Current

Riding the waves with a whoop and a cheer,
While the water splashes, followed by beer.
A dolphin winks, gives a funny grin,
As we hope for a win, but tumble in!

Current carries us, all laughter and cheers,
With beach towels flying, oh dear, oh dear!
A kid on a floatie, all glory and pride,
Just toppled over, what a slippery ride!

Waves swirl around like a dance of the fools,
We dive and we laugh, breaking all the rules.
Floating and flopping, our worries drift far,
Under the watch of the sun and a star.

So here we float, in the water so wide,
With smiles so contagious, we take it in stride.
The current embraces our giggles and dreams,
In this splashy paradise, nothing's as it seems.

Ripples of Peace

Waves crash and laugh at my toes,
Starfish giggle, in funny prose.
Seagulls squawk, wearing shades too,
Nature's humor, oh, what a view.

Flip-flops fly, oh what a sight,
Chasing crabs, I'm in for a fight.
A jellyfish whispers, "Take it slow,"
While I trip and land—a comedy show.

Sandcastles wobble, I cheer from afar,
A moat for my throne, but it's perilous by far.
Buckets and shovels, mischief in hand,
Building a fortress of flung grains of sand.

But in the end, as the tide rolls back,
I chuckle and sip from my juice-stained pack.
For peace here is found in the laughter we share,
While the ocean's waves tickle the salty air.

Solitude Beneath the Stars

Lying on blankets, the stars overhead,
Counting constellations, in dreams we are fed.
A crab scuttles close, with plans to invade,
But my snack's looking tasty, so I'm not afraid.

The moon smirks down, surveying the scene,
As I debate if that shadow's a bean.
A fish jumps out, and it leaves quite a splash,
Making me giggle while I try not to thrash.

In the quiet nights, laughter slinks near,
A raccoon sneaks by, and I wrestle my fear.
We share this calm, under shimmering light,
With silly thoughts dancing, oh what a sight!

And just as I drift into slumber's embrace,
A chorus of creatures fills up the space.
Solitude sings in the calm of the night,
With laughter and stars, everything feels right.

Nautical Reverie

A boat bobbles up, like it's playing a game,
With fish jumping out, vying for fame.
Sailors hoot loudly, telling tall tales,
As octopuses giggle, unfurling their scales.

The wind starts to tease, knots in my hair,
As I pretend to steer, without a care.
A seagull lands, wanting to share,
It squawks, "Dude, let's fly! Why sit in this chair?"

Turtles swim by, give me a stare,
Like, "What's with that hat? Did your friend dare?"
Fish in the deep start a bubble parade,
While mermaids join in, throwing confetti, I'm afraid.

But in this sea far from the land,
Life floats along, just as we planned.
Together we sail on a wave of delight,
In this nautical dream, everything feels right.

Melody of the Seagulls

Seagulls sing out in a comical way,
Competing for snacks, like it's their play.
I throw them a fry; they squawk and they dive,
With antics so wild, they're truly alive.

The beach ball rolls past, like a runaway fool,
While kids chase it down, splashing in the pool.
The ocean chuckles, holding back its roar,
As laughter rings out, who could ask for more?

A pirate ship sails, but it leans a bit left,
With crew members giggling, oh what a theft!
They shout for their treasure, but it's just a snack,
While I munch on my chips, and thrive in the lack.

As the sun dips low, painting skies bright,
Seagulls are singing, it's pure delight.
In this funny world, where joy spills like beer,
A melody plays that brings everyone near.

Reflections on the Waters

Waves giggle and splash, oh what a sight,
Fish wear sunglasses, swimming in delight.
Seagulls are jesters, with jokes to share,
And crabs are tap dancing, without a care.

Sandcastles wobble, they twist and they sway,
A bucket of laughter, sunshine at play.
Seashells whisper tales, oh so absurd,
Of octopuses playing, inquiring if they've heard.

Fishermen chuckle, reeling in jest,
One's got a shoe, proclaiming it best.
While dolphins do flips, and flip flops just fly,
Leaving everyone giggling, waving goodbye.

Footprints in the sand, a comic parade,
Doodles of feet where memories are laid.
Nature's chuckle, a curious tease,
As laughter drifts softly, carried by breeze.

Moonlit Musings by the Coast

Under the moonlight, the beach tells a tale,
Of crabs in pajamas, and fish that sail.
Starfish gossip loudly, in vocal delight,
While waves play the drums, in the cool of the night.

The moon winks down, with a silvery grin,
And jellyfish jiggle, just itching to swim.
Seagulls hold court, debating their food,
While the ocean's a stage, in a whimsical mood.

On this sandy expanse, giggles abound,
As mermaids tell stories, profound and round.
Ambitious octopi juggle starry props,
In the glow of the moonlight, laughter just hops.

Mirthful reflections, on water like glass,
Where waves giggle softly, and shadows all pass.
The night is alive with a fun-loving breeze,
As creatures rejoice, beneath cosmic trees.

The Calm Between Storms

Before the tempest, there's a silence sweet,
Where gulls take a break, and crabs dance on feet.
The tide whispers secrets, in a half-hearted breeze,
As sandcastles tremble, at nature's tease.

In the distance, clouds bicker, but here it's all fun,
With turtles on surfboards, basking in sun.
Frolicking waves, with gelato to share,
As the shoreline chuckles, shedding its care.

Footprints of laughter, trace out a dance,
While sea cucumbers flirt, in their undersea romance.
The calm is a prank, before chaos ensues,
A light-hearted pause, like a well-timed muse.

And when storms do arrive, let them roll and roar,
For we'll build a fort, and merrily soar.
In the calm between bursts, let's revel and gleam,
Life's just a movie—a ridiculous dream!

Pebbles and Footprints

Pebbles like giggles, scattered on the shore,
Each tells a story, of fun days before.
Footprints dance onward, skipping with glee,
While waves crack a joke, oh, come join the spree!

The sea's full of mischief, secrets in the tide,
With crabby comedians, grinning side to side.
Every splash makes a sound, like laughter so bright,
As starfish flip pages of the ocean's night.

Mollusks are mischievous, poorly disguised,
Playing hide-and-seek, oh, how they have pried!
Little ones giggle, as gulls swoop and dive,
Life on the beach is where joy's kept alive.

Hold tight to your smiles, let the fun be your guide,
For pebbles and footprints hold stories inside.
In the salty air, laughter finder our way,
Silliness reigns, on this bright sunny day.

A Haven of Calm

Waves crashing like a joke that fell flat,
A seagull squawks, 'I stole your sandwich, chitchat!'
The sun wears sunglasses, looking quite cool,
While crabs play chess, breaking every rule.

Beach balls bounce, a pirate's old dream,
Sandcastle scandals, hear the seagulls scream.
Kids digging treasures, finding lost socks,
While turtles tweet from their sandy docks.

Buckets and shovels, playful toolkits,
Who knew at the beach, you'd need a few wits?
The ocean's a trickster, waves laugh and swirl,
Come join the fun, let your worries unfurl.

As sun sets on laughter, and evenings grow bright,
Shells telling stories, in fading daylight.
A haven of giggles, where sand meets the tide,
Life's just a playground—so come for the ride!

Secrets of the Shore

Whispers of laughter dance on the breeze,
Where volleyball's served with a side of cheese.
Crabs in tuxedos, stroll with great flair,
While starfish gossip, 'Who wore it better, beware?'

Shells hold secrets, they just won't tell,
One claims it's a treasure, the other, a shell!
Kids build a fortress, it's made of pure sand,
While a seagull surveys, like a royal grand.

Flip-flops abandoned, lost in the race,
But worries float off like foam on the face.
A beach bag of snacks, a treasure so grand,
With sandwiches laughing, at jelly so bland.

The tide comes in, with jokes that rebuke,
Sandy footprints spell out, 'Start up a fluke!'
A rhythm of giggles as night softly creeps,
At the edge of the world, where laughter never sleeps.

Moonlight on Gentle Waters

The moon winks brightly, a prankster at sea,
Casting shadows of fish, all wiggly and free.
Starfish throw parties, inviting the night,
While mermaids sing karaoke, in pure delight.

On boats little critters are rockin' away,
Paddling furiously, like they're in a ballet.
Gulls photobomb images, strutting with glee,
As crabs choreograph dances, oh look at me!

The waves hum a tune, a catchy new beat,
While seaweed sways gently, tapping its feet.
Jellyfish glow softly, glow sticks in hand,
Ready to sparkle at this beach-side grand.

Under the stars, the ocean's big laugh,
With no fish on duty, let joy be your staff.
Moonlight giggles, as morning takes flight,
A comedy show, all through the night!

The Dance of Seashells

Seashells in a circle, holding a jam,
With conch blowing trumpets, and clams doing glam.
Crabs in a conga, legs moving so fast,
Inviting all sea life to join in the blast.

Sand dollars sulking, quite envious they are,
Wanting a spotlight, wishing on a star.
Clownfish crack jokes, with bubbles and glee,
While octopuses juggle, look at me, look at me!

Rainbow fish twirl, as they brighten the sea,
Their scales glimmer golden, a sight jubilee.
Underwater laughter bubbles up with the tides,
As the current picks up, where rhythm abides.

Under the moonlight, they dance the night long,
A quirky ocean festival, with laughter, a song.
Seashells keep rocking, the beach floor they claim,
With a wave and a wink, they'll never be the same!

The Quiet Call of the Deep

Waves crash and giggle, oh what a sound,
Seagulls squawking, they gather around.
Barefoot and laughing, I dance in the sand,
A crab on my toe, slapstick is planned.

Buckets and shovels, our tools for the day,
Building a castle, in a comical way.
But as the tide rises, our dreams start to sink,
Defeated by water, we pause to think.

We throw all our cares to the foam on the shore,
While jellyfish bob and then wiggle some more.
Oh, what a circus, with fish taking flight,
As I tumble and roll, much to my delight.

A seaweed crown tops this silly parade,
In this quirky kingdom, our worries do fade.
So join in the laughter, let joy set the tone,
The ocean's embrace feels like coming back home.

Harboring Peace

There's a seagull who squawks with laughter and glee,
Every time he spots a fish swimming free.
I chuckle as tides play hide and seek,
My sunscreen melts, oh what a cheek!

My beach towel's a map of sand-centered dreams,
As I chase after ice cream, unbothered it seems.
With each sticky scoop, I'm lost in delight,
While a sly little dog gives my snack a big bite.

I dive in the waves, think I'll find treasure,
But it's just a flip-flop, oh what a measure!
The moon sets to dance, a disco at sea,
Seashells are my tickets to the party with me.

So here's to the giggles, the fun and the sun,
Where every small mishap is just part of the fun.
The day drifts to whispers, as stars start to peek,
With laughter as my compass, the future looks sleek.

Beyond the Breaking Surf

A surfboard appears, and the crowd lets out cheer,
But I'm splashed in the face by a wave of cold beer.
With landing all shaky, like a fish out of sea,
Jumping back on my board, oh is that a bee?

I navigate foam like a raccoon in night,
With my arms flailing wildly, it's a comic sight.
The lifeguard chuckles, a hero in red,
As I twirl and I crash, it's pure joy, I said.

The sun beams above, with laughter I'll boast,
As I chase after waves, I become their host.
In the chaos of splashes and humorous rides,
I find joy in my tumbles, and my fun-loving slides.

So let's raise a toast to the capsizing crew,
For every odd tumble, there's laughter anew.
On this surfboard of life, let the giggles be heard,
As we ride through each wave, with laughter's sweet word.

A Sanctuary of Seagrass

In the seaweed forest, I dance with a crab,
He waves his small claws like a live sea-club.
I trip on a rock, my splash sends a spray,
As fish jump for joy, in a fishy ballet.

The starfish just giggles, he's got nothing to do,
While I'm lost in the chaos, of beach walk and brew.
With seagulls as judges, they applaud my ballet,
But my flip-flops are missing, oh what a display!

Seagrass sways gently, like dancers in line,
As I stumble and tumble, a cute little sign.
Let's play hide and seek with the shells on the shore,
Finding treasures and giggles, who could want more?

So gather your laughter, your joy, and your cheer,
For each wave that rolls in brings the world near.
With a wink from the sea, we wink back and play,
In this sanctuary of whimsy, we'll dance all day.

Echoing Breezes

The seagulls squawk, they take a dive,
Trying to steal my snack, oh how they strive!
With waves that crash and tickle my toes,
I giggle out loud as the ocean just glows.

The winds like clowns, they dance and play,
Flipping my hat, then whisking away.
Each splash is a joke, a watery jest,
And I can't help but laugh, it's a humorous fest.

Sandcastles built with a wobbly base,
Fall down like my dreams in this crazy race.
As children giggle and splash all around,
I find my own laughter in each silly sound.

So here I will stay, where the fun never ends,
With echoes of humor from sea to my friends.
We'll chase the sunset with laughter and glee,
At this beach of jest, just my friends and me.

Twilight by the Sea

The sun dips low, and soon it's night,
With shadows that dance, it's quite a sight.
Crabs in tuxedos, a fancy parade,
Strutting their stuff, their claws never fade.

The waves start to giggle, they tickle my feet,
As jellyfish float, in a strange little beat.
I point at a starfish, "Is that your big toe?"
And everyone laughs, 'cause it steals the show.

The twilight brings whispers from shells on the shore,
"Tell us a joke!" they eagerly implore.
With each little wave and each grain of sand,
The humor flows freely; it's truly unplanned.

And thus, I shall laugh, at the sea's silly ways,
In this twilight of chuckles, I'll spend all my days.
With a heart full of joy and a smile on my face,
I embrace the night's laughter, it's my happy place.

Sunlit Serenity

In sunlit rays, the beach looks bright,
Kids scream and shout, it's a funny sight.
With buckets and spades, they're building their dreams,
While chasing the waves and creating strange schemes.

A dog in the water, a fish on the run,
Trying to fetch, oh what fun has begun!
Waves crash around, like they're in a race,
Yet, it's just the dog's epic splashing face.

Umbrellas are tumbling, they dance in a spin,
As beach balls are flying like they too want in.
I spot a sunbather, who's lost in a book,
He'll jump with surprise, if the seagulls should cook.

With laughter a-bubbling and sunshine on skin,
We gather our giggles, let the fun never thin.
For every wave's whisper, and every sunbeam,
Brings forth the humor that feels like a dream.

Golden Sands of Tranquility

On golden sands, the adults unwind,
While children throw tantrums, oh aren't they kind?
A bucket spills water with a silly splash,
As parents just smile, hiding their clash.

A beach ball soars high, it thinks it's a star,
But lands with a thud, oh dear, that's bizarre!
With laughter erupting like bubbles in air,
We cheer on the poor ball, it's quite the affair.

Sand between toes, like tickly little ants,
Makes everyone giggle, even while they prance.
"Let's make a picnic!" a wise one suggests,
Only to find snacks crushed in a mess.

But here on this shore, amidst laughter and cheer,
How funny life's moments can really appear.
So here we shall stay, with joy in our sight,
In this golden cocoon, everything feels right.

Pathways in the Sand

Footprints in the sand, oh what a mess,
Seagulls laugh, they surely confess.
With each wave that comes crashing by,
I trip on a shell, and oh my, oh my!

Tide rolls in, it gives me a shove,
Floats me like a feather, I'm a free little dove.
But here comes the crab, he scuttles so quick,
I dance a jig, oh what a funny flick!

Kites in the sky, they go up and spin,
I try to look cool, but it's hard to win.
The wind takes my hat, straight off my head,
And now it's a game of who gets fed!

Together we laugh, the beach folk unite,
Waves crash and tumble, what a joyful sight.
With sandy mishaps and bits to recall,
Life is just better when you stumble and fall!

Breath of the Coastal Wind

With a whiff of salt, the breeze floats near,
It messes my hair; look, I'm a seafarer!
Flip-flops flip as we stroll along,
Laughter erupts—there's always a song!

The breeze whispers sweetly, 'Let's fly a kite!'
It takes off like magic, oh what a sight!
But my sandwich snatched, now where did it go?
The gulls are just crafty, as crafty can show.

Waves rush in, they tickle my toes,
Dancing with foam, oh how it goes!
I jump with delight as I slip and I slide,
Can't tell if I'm swimming or surfing the tide!

With warmth on my skin and a chuckle or two,
We're all a big family, that much is true.
So here's to the wind, the sand, and the fun,
Life's a beach party, and we've all just begun!

Celestial Shores

Stars twinkle bright, like diamonds on glass,
Falling in laughter, moments so vast.
With stories of beaches and silly old tales,
We chuckle aloud as we chase down the whales.

An octopus winks, oh what a surprise,
He juggles fish bowls, and to our demise,
I slipped off my flip-flop, it floated away,
I guess it's now playing a game of 'heyday'!

Moonlight gleams on where we sit tight,
We're snacking on popcorn; oh, what a sight!
Seashells like pillows, we lay on the shore,
Silly little crabs join us, wanting some more!

With each wave that splashes, we echo our cheer,
In a world full of wonders, there's nothing to fear.
So grab your friends and let out a roar,
At these celestial shores, we forever explore!

Harmony in the Depths

Underwater wonders, where bubbles ignite,
I snorkeled with dolphins, in pure delight.
But what's that? A fish just swam by,
Wearing a bowtie—oh my, oh my!

A turtle named Timmy just winked at me,
As he rolled by silently, happy and free.
I tried to do flips, but was caught in a whirl,
Turns out swimming's not my best twirl!

Coral of colors, it's a candy land dream,
I met a sea star who started to beam.
"Join in the fun, let's boogie on down!"
But first a sea urchin gave me a frown.

We all find our rhythm in silly old ways,
Dancing with fish in their playful displays.
So here's to the depths and the giggles we keep,
Life's a splash of joy, the ocean's a leap!

www.ingramcontent.com/pod-product-compliance
Lightning Source LLC
Chambersburg PA
CBHW072134070526
44585CB00016B/1671